ALSO BY ZUNI BLUE

Ninja Poo Gets Revenge
The Mean Girl Who Never Speaks
The Missing Hamster Who Didn't Escape

ZUNI BLUE

HOW TO WRITE AMAZING STORIES
10 CREATIVE WRITING TIPS FOR YOUNG WRITERS

ALL-SEEING BOOKS
LONDON

First published in 2015 by All-Seeing Books
www.all-seeingbooks.com

Cover Photo Copyright © Dazdraperma/bigstockphoto.com

ISBN-13: 978-1519163523
ISBN-10: 1519163525

CONTENTS

This book is written in British English.

How To Write Amazing Stories

Hi, I'm Zuni Blue!

I write books for kids. I started writing stories at a young age, just like you! It was so much fun to imagine my own worlds. Reading other people's stories is great, but don't you wonder what story you could write?

Now you can find out...

This mini-guide has the 10 steps that'll take you from a blank page to lots of stories. Lots of people start stories but never finish them because writing seems scary.

It's not, really.

Just follow each step. Spend at least a whole week on each part and then move on. If you need more time, slow down. You've got your whole writing career ahead of you. No need to rush!

Step 1: Find Your Work Space

There are so many distractions, especially when it's time to write! Your brother might put the TV on. Your sister might play loud music. Your dad starts DIY. Then your mum cooks food that smells really good.

It's like they're doing it on purpose!

Actually, they're not. They probably did those things before, so why is it so irritating now?

Because you're trying to focus.

When you try really hard to concentrate, other things irritate you. Even tiny things like the birds chirping outside or the kids playing next door.

Then you might be a bit grouchy. You say something mean, hurting someone you care about. Or get yourself in trouble...

It's not just other people who distract you.

You might too.

That new video game Dad bought you. The dolls you got for your birthday. Sweets from the local store. Funny websites online. Your favourite TV show. A new pop tune by your favourite band. When it's time to write, all your other favourite things want your attention too!

Distractions are a big problem for writers.

So, what's the solution?

Find your own work space.

One of the great things about being a writer is writing anywhere in the world. You could be on a sunny beach on holiday, walking through the countryside or even at home in bed. This means we have lots of work space to choose from. As long as we get quiet time, it'll do.

Look around the house and garden for a spot where you can work in peace.

When you've found the right spot, test it out. Is it quiet? Even better, is it silent? Can you at least hear yourself think?

Light is very important. If you write in a dark place, you'll strain your eyes. Your eyes do a lot for you, so take care of them. Make sure there's a lamp over your work space. Natural light from the sun is another option.

Are you comfortable? Is there space to stretch out, walk about on your breaks, and step away from your story to think? Don't squeeze into tight spots or go into dangerous places. Your work space should always be safe.

Is your work space already taken? Maybe your dad needs his desk for work. Maybe your sister needs the bathroom to do her make-up. Maybe your brother needs the garden for his sports training. Ask your family if they need the work space.

Don't worry if the spot is taken. You've got a whole week to find the right spot. Don't rush it.

The most important point is: Do your parents/carers know where you are? Like I said, your writing space should be safe. Your parents should know where you are. Let them check over your spot. They might help make it even better.

Great! Now you've got a private, quiet work space just for you. Everyone knows that's where you work, and they'll respect your space.

Now for some fun...

Decorate your work space. Stick up cool pictures of places and people you'd like to write about. You might play some background music. Not too loud or it'll distract you. Some writers have photos of authors they'd like to be like.

Whatever you do, make sure your work space is YOURS. Don't copy others. Be yourself.

Now you've got your own office it's time to decide how often you'll write.

Step 2: Plan Your Schedule

Do you want writing to be a hobby (something you do for fun) or a job (in the future)? All young writers should start out just having fun. If you enjoy something now, you can always earn a living from it later.

Just because you're having fun, doesn't mean you can't set a writing target. Without a target it's easy to skip writing sessions. You think, "Yeah, I'll do it tomorrow..." then tomorrow comes and you skip writing again. By having a writing goal you can stay on track.

What is your ultimate writing goal? Don't know? I didn't either until I answered the following three questions:

How many days will you spend writing each week?

How much time do you have each day?

How many words do you want to write each day?

Now let's focus on each question.

1. How many days will you spend writing each week?

It's best to start small and work up from there, for example, if your ultimate goal is to write five days a week, it's okay to start with one or two. Once you've managed your little goal, add more days.

2. How much time do you have each day?

Writing your story should come after your homework and chores. Always. After you've finished them, how much time do you have left? Set aside some time to play - you deserve it after a long day at school - and use your spare time to write. It doesn't matter if you've got ten minutes or an hour. Just commit to your writing time until you finish the story.

3. How many words do you want to write each day?

Professional writers might write as much as ten thousand words a day or as low as a hundred. It depends on how much time you have. The more time you have, the more you can write. It doesn't matter if you write less than someone else. This isn't a competition. Just pick a word count you're comfortable with and see what happens.

I recommend starting small. Why not try writing at least three sentences a day? Once you meet that target, aim higher. If you don't meet your target, it doesn't matter. Keep trying your best every day. Some days you'll write more. Some days you'll write less. Just keep having fun!

All the answers you gave to those questions will build up to your ultimate goal.

Don't expect to meet your long-term goal right away. It'll take time. It might take days, weeks or even months. It doesn't matter. Just focus on enjoying your story. Keep going until it's done.

Before we start planning or writing anything, there is one VERY, VERY important step. If you skip it, you might lose your stories forever.

Step 3: Back-up! Back-up! Back-up!

It's very, very, very important that you back-up your work. Millions upon millions of words are lost every year because writers didn't back-up their work.

There are several ways to lose your work: someone might damage your computer by accident, your computer might get a virus, or you might lose your work somewhere. Don't panic! By backing up your work you'll make sure that you never lose your work.

Now you've decided to back-up your work, I need you to promise me something: you'll back-up every time you write. I know, I know. It seems like a chore, but you'll thank me if you ever lose your work. By backing-up every time you write you'll make sure you never lose a day's work. If you back-up once a week, you'll lose days of work. If you back-up once a month, you'll lose hundreds of words and several chapters.

Oh, and another promise: you'll back-up in more than one place. This means if one back-up gets lost or destroyed, you'll have another copy elsewhere. An easy way to back-up in more than place is by emailing to different email addresses. Why not email a copy to your mum and dad's email addresses? That's two copies already!

Email is one way to back-up a copy of your work. Printing off a copy is another way to keep a back-up, but keep your print-outs in two different places, for example, keep one at your house and another at your grandparents' house.

Another way to back-up is by saving your work on a storage device. A storage device includes CDs, USB sticks, hard drives, and cloud drives.

If you save work on CDs, make sure you keep them in sturdy cases and try not to scratch the CDs.

If you use USBs, keep them somewhere safe or you'll lose them. I suggest keeping them near the computer when you're writing - it'll remind you to back-up your work.

Hard drives aren't cheap, but they've got lots of space. Why not share it with your family? Then no one will lose their work.

Cloud drives are online storage. You'll need your parents to open an account for you. Email addresses often come with cloud storage, so your parents probably have cloud storage already. Just ask them to back-up your work on their account.

If you're still not sure about backing up your work, please just do it. Imagine losing all the stories you've written. All the characters, worlds, and amazing tales will be gone. Sure you can start again, but it won't be the same. Trust me, it hurts to lose your work. I cried like a baby.

If you think it's no big deal to lose your work, I dare you to go and delete it all off right now. Start every story all over again. Go on. Yeah, didn't think so. Just the thought of starting again is nerve-wracking. If you're really unlucky, you'll lose YEARS of work.

It's up to you.

Now that your work is safe, it's time to create the star of your story.

Step 4: Create Your Characters

This is a very important part of writing. Your characters are a big part of your story. Readers will love 'em or hate 'em. How readers feel about each character is your decision. It all depends on how the character acts, looks, and feels.

Here are five major parts of your character you should consider:

1. Important Details.

Three really important details to choose first are age, gender and a name.

A key detail is age. If your character is a child, there's certain things they won't be allowed to do o.g. got a job. They'll be at school instead. If your character is old, they won't be as active as a younger person.

Because you're young, it might be best to stick with young characters. Then you can write about all the stuff you go through as a kid. Think of your own life and turn it into a great story!

Now you've decided what age your character is, time to pick their gender. Is your character a girl or a boy? A man or a woman? As a new writer, it'll be easier writing as your own gender.

Gender will influence your character a lot, for example, boys in stories might have more action than girls. Other stuff that varies depending on gender includes their clothes, hair, toys, and how they react to their problems.

After choosing an age and gender, choosing a name is also fun! You can use the name of someone you really know, your own name, or even a famous person's. For more of a challenge, look up the meaning of names. Does the meaning fit your story? Does the name fit your character's personality, for example, would you call an evil witch Sasha or Fluffy?

You can pick just a first name or choose a full name. It's up to you. If you've never written before, start with just a first name. With more writing practise and experience, give your characters full names too e.g. Jane can become Jane Ashley Jones.

2. Appearance.

How does your character look? You could draw the character or describe them in words. Just make sure you've got a description to refer to as you write.

Is your character tall or short or in between?

What race is your character?

What kind of hair do they have? Do they have any facial hair like a beard? What colour is their hair?

What do they smell like?

What does their voice sound like?

What clothes and shoes do they wear?

Answer those questions to get a general idea of what the character looks like.

3. Personality.

Personality will determine how your character acts, what they say and do, and even who they hang around with. What is your character like? Choosing a personality isn't easy. Here are some questions to help you out.

Are they mean or nice?

Are they good or bad?

Do they have any bad habits e.g. bite their nails a lot?

Are they noisy or quiet?

Are they loners or sociable?

Are they serious or funny?

Do you want readers to like them or dislike them?

Remember that you can combine personality types. No one is good or bad all the time. You can always change how they act depending on the situation they're in, for example, a nice, shy girl might be angry and mean to her older brother because he broke her favourite doll.

4. Flaws.

Great stories show how a character changes over time, for example, a mean character might be nicer at the end. No one is perfect, so your character shouldn't be either. Flaws are things we'd like to change about ourselves. So, what's wrong with your character?

Are they too mean? Too nice?

Too nervous? Too confident?

Too lazy? Or maybe they never sit still?

Do they eat too much?

Maybe they never share?

There are so many flaws out there. By the end of the story, your character might have overcome their flaws. For example, if your character is very shy at the start, readers will be happy when she comes out of her shell at the end. That's why it's useful to think of the opposite of each flaw, for example, the opposite of eating too many sweets is eating lovely fruits instead.

5. Family, Friends and Foes.

Consider who your character lives with, and also write down a little about each family member. It doesn't have to be detailed, especially if the character isn't in the story, but include some info for future stories. You never know if that character will appear in a story later.

Does your character have parents?

Does your character have brothers and sisters?

Do they have a pet?

Who is your character's best friend?

Do they have a girlfriend or boyfriend?

Who is your character's arch enemy?

You could draw a family tree showing your character and all their family, and do another one for their friends. When you describe family members, try to make them sound similar to your main character. Then it'll be more realistic.

Great! You've got lots of great characters to write about. One problem, though. They need somewhere to live...

Step 5: Create Your World

Now you've chosen your characters, they'll need a world to live in. You have two options: they can live in our world or a fictional world you created.

Basing your story in the real world is a popular option. You can include real attractions like the Statue of Liberty in New York, or Big Ben in London. Why not set your story in your hometown? Then you can show the world how cool your hometown is. If you say nice things about them, you can even use real people. Don't say anything mean or they'll get upset.

The second option is creating a world from scratch. You get to choose everything from the planet to the types of people, or aliens, there. If you create your own world, consider the following:

What time period is it? Past, present or future?

Which planet is it set on? A real one or a fictional one?

What is the climate like? Is it hot, cold, sunny, snowy, wet or dry?

Are your characters living on a continent or an island?

Will you set your story in a country, a city or a town?

What places are there to visit e.g. a zoo, a park, a theme park, a beach, etc?

What races are there in your world? By races I mean two things. Races can mean white, black, Asian or biracial people. It can also mean human, elf, wizard, etc.

You can also draw your setting. It's fun drawing a map of where your characters live. It's also useful when you start writing because you'll remember where everyone is.

As you can see, creating a world is lots of fun. If you're not sure what to choose, just start writing and see what happens. And remember that you can always change your mind later. Or your characters can travel to lots of different lands. Then you get to write about lots of different places and the different races who live there.

Now you've got your characters and a world, it's time to start planning your story...

Step 6: Plan Your Story

Before you read this chapter, let me just say that planning your story is optional. Some people work best when they just start writing. Others enjoy planning and having the story mapped out in advance. To find out what kind of writer you are, try both. Stick with the method you prefer.

Planning a story isn't hard. All you need is a beginning, middle and end. What happens in between doesn't matter right now. Your imagination will fill in the blanks when you're writing.

1. The Beginning.

To plan a beginning, all you have to do is show how your character starts their story. Consider the following questions:

Where do they live?

Who do they live with?

Are they happy?

Is there anything that might stop them being happy?

What are your character's dreams and goals?

2. The End.

To plan an ending, all you have to do is show the opposite of the beginning. Here are some examples.

Example 1

At the start, a little girl is bored with her life.

At the end, she's been on an adventure and is happy to be back home.

Example 2

At the start, a boy lives in a world controlled by an evil wizard.

At the end, the boy's defeated the wizard and the world is happy again.

Example 3

At the start, a mouse is far away from home and lost.

At the end, he's found his family and friends, and is happy at home.

See? The end is just the opposite of the beginning. Sadness turns to happiness. A major threat is defeated. Dreams come true. Goals are met. Happy ever after...unless there's a sequel!

3. The Middle.

The middle is also easy to plan for. All you have to do is make life difficult for your characters, then get them out of trouble. For example, that lost mouse I mentioned earlier might meet an evil cat, but escape to safety. Then the mouse might get stuck in a mouse trap, but a friendly boy might set him free. See how bad stuff happens but then everything works out? That's your middle.

The best writers make sure the bad stuff get worse as the story progresses to the end. It builds up excitement for readers until the big finale. Then everything is all right and the character can sit back and relax.

Remember, you don't need to plan every little thing. Too much planning makes writing boring. You feel like you've got to stick to the plan. Then when you think of cool things you'd like to write, you don't because they're not in the plan. So don't plan the first story. Just enjoy the experience. For your second story, try planning. Then compare the two. Which one was fun (or more fun)? Which story was better? Ask others for feedback. The final decision is yours. If you can't decide, no big deal. You can do both if you want.

Okay, you've decided whether to plan your story or not. Now it's time for the best part of being an author: you get to write!

Step 7: Write

The best part. Go to your writing spot and write. It doesn't matter if you're putting pen to paper or fingers to the keyboard. All you do is start writing and let the story out. If you've got a plan ready, look over the start to see what's happening next. If you don't want to plan, that's fine too. Just start writing and see what happens.

Here's some advice before you start.

1. Be Yourself.

Sometimes other people try to write your story for you. They make suggestions or rewrite your work - don't let them. This is your story. You decide what happens. When others jump in, it can confuse you. It can make you doubt yourself. Don't worry. Just keep writing until you reach the end.

2. Regular Breaks.

Because writers use their hands a lot, it's very important to take regular breaks so you don't hurt your hands and eyes. A general guideline I follow is stopping every fifteen to thirty minutes. Some writers go for an hour.

When you stop, stretch your body, walk on the spot for a minute or so, and then do something else e.g. use the toilet, get a snack, get a drink, etc. After five to ten minutes, come back and keep writing.

3. No Rules.

Writing only seems hard when writers follow lots of rules. They think you can't do certain things when you write because your teacher tells you not to at school. They're wrong.

When you do your school work, follow the rules. Don't get into trouble.

When you write stories for yourself, do whatever you like. You can start sentences with 'and'. You can use lots of commas or a little. You can write a new sentence on each line. When you write stories, perfect sentences don't matter as long as your story is good.

And it will be.

Just follow that advice and you should be fine.

Now go and write!

Step 8: Edit Your Work

Now your work is done, it's time to edit it. Editing involves fixing mistakes and anything that doesn't make sense. It's best to edit after some time away from your work. In the meantime, write your next story. When you're done, come back.

When you edit, look out for certain things:

1. Punctuation.

Full stops, commas, exclamation marks, and question marks.

2. Similar Words.

Their and there, see and sea, here and hear.

3. Confusion.

Does each sentence and paragraph make sense? If not, rewrite.

Now it's time to decide how you'll edit. Look over the following methods. You could try all of them if you like. You can do more than one type of edit on each story, but don't edit too much. Too much editing and rewriting can ruin a good story.

Here are some editing methods that professionals use. Choose at least one.

1. Read Slowly.

This one is simple. All you do is read the story slowly from start to finish. This gives you extra time to catch mistakes you'd miss reading quickly. If you read slowly then you only need to edit once. Your beta reader can catch anything you missed.

To practise reading slowly, read a word per second. If you don't have a watch, just pause between each word. If that's too slow for you, you can speed it up. If it's too fast, slow down. It's totally up to you!

The problem is that slow reading can be a bit boring. It drags on sometimes. Plus there's no guarantee you'll catch more mistakes by reading slowly.

2. Read Quickly.

You just read the book a bit faster than you normally would. It's like skim-reading. If you don't like reading slowly then this option might be for you.

The problem with reading quickly is that you're going so fast that you might miss more mistakes. Because of this, I recommend reading through twice. This gives you two chances to spot mistakes.

3. Print Off and Read.

All you do is print off the story and read it. Some people feel they spot mistakes easier this way because it looks different from the computer monitor. It's also good because it gives your eyes a break from looking at the screen too long. Another bonus is that you can annotate the work with highlighters and pens.

This option costs more money because you'll be using lots of ink and paper. Always check there's enough paper and ink before you print. You can also change the printer settings so the book comes out like a book. Then you can glue the pages together, or ask your parents to staple it together for you.

4. Read On-screen.

This is cheaper than printing off your story. The story is already on the computer. All you have to do is open the document and start reading. You can highlight text using the program you wrote on. Another bonus is that you can correct mistakes straight away.

The downside is that your eyes don't get a break from staring at the computer screen. And your hands don't get a proper break from using the keyboard.

5. Read Aloud.

You read the book aloud. You could read it by yourself, to your family or your friends. Your teacher might let you read some at school. Reading out loud helps catch mistakes because when you read in your head, your brain might correct mistakes without you knowing.

When you're done editing, give the book to your beta reader. Beta readers are people who read the book for you. They give feedback on what they liked, and tell you about any mistakes they found. Anyone can be a beta reader including family and friends.

Don't obsess over finding mistakes. Even famous best-sellers have mistakes in their books. Readers know mistakes happen. They won't hold it against you. It won't stop them from reading your next book. So don't worry if you and your beta reader miss a mistake or two.

Just do your best.

Phew! That covers editing. What else does your book need? A cover!

Step 9: Design Your Cover

Every book needs a cover! You can do it on the computer or on paper. Paper is much more fun because you can use different tools like paint, crayons, colouring pens and other art materials. The more creative you are the better. And doing it yourself means you can guarantee no one has a cover like yours.

When you design your cover, consider the following:

1. Genre.

Examples of genres are horror, crime, fantasy and romance. The best book covers show the book's genre. Then readers who like that genre will read it. If you're not sure what pictures fit your book's genre, look around the library. Usually the genre is obvious, for example, a fantasy book cover might have a dragon on it. A crime book might have a detective. A horror book might have a ghost. If you're not sure, you can always pick your main character instead.

2. BIG Name.

Famous best-selling authors' names are always really big on the cover. Readers know a big name means the author is a popular writer, so they give the book a chance.

I know you're just getting started, but that doesn't mean your name should be small. Make it really big! Let your name take up around a third of the book cover. When your family and friends see how big it is, they'll be really impressed.

3. BIG Title.

When books are on the bookshelf, it's very important that you can read the title. Then it'll catch people's eyes when they walk by. And, like with having a big name, it makes you look like a professional, best-selling author from the start. Very impressive!

4. Cool Pictures.

Picking a picture for your cover is the best part. You could draw your character so people know what they look like. Or cut out pictures from magazines and stick them down. Or draw a nice background with paint, pens, or crayons. You could even use the computer instead. If you like taking pictures, you could take some nice ones that fit your book, for example, if your book is about a dog, take a picture of your dog and put him/her on the cover.

5. Yes or No.

Do you like it? You can ask others, but it's your book. Do *you* like the cover? Does anything stand out for the wrong reasons? Maybe the title is too small. Maybe your name isn't clear. Maybe the picture doesn't fit what your book is about.

To find out what's stopping you from liking the cover, try this: look away from the cover, now look at the cover. What gets your attention first? Is it for a good reason or a bad one? If it's bad, change it and see how you feel after a second look. Repeat the exercise until you like everything.

Look at the covers of books you love. What do you like about the cover? Is it the colours? Is it the picture? When you look at the cover, what's the first thing you notice? You'll pick up great tips for your own book.

When you like the cover, great! You should be very proud of yourself. The last part of publishing the book is done.

Now it's time to find readers.

Step 10: Find Readers

Now you've got your books done, it's time to find an audience. There are millions of readers out there, but because you're so young it's best to start small. A small audience means much less pressure and lots of time to improve your skills.

The first great place to find readers is at home. Your family will happily read your work for you. They'll be so proud of your work and commitment. You should be proud of yourself too!

The second place to find readers is your group of friends. You could even swap work you've done. Why not have a writers' sleepover? You could brainstorm story ideas, discuss great books you've read, give each other useful, positive feedback, and then chill out with other fun stuff like watching cartoons or playing video games.

Another place to find readers is at school. If you're comfortable doing it, read your work to the class. Don't be sad if any feedback is negative - that's normal. All writers get bad reviews. If you agree with the criticism, you can change your work. If you disagree, leave your work as it is. It is your book and your career, so always make sure you have the final say.

One more place to find readers is in your hometown. Writers love to read, so check the library at school. You'll definitely find writers there. Also ask the librarian if there are any great writing books to read. While you're there, why not suggest a book club or writing competition. Winning isn't important, but getting involved in the writing community is.

You can also visit your local library. Ask your parents to take you to a book club for adults. Then you can see professional writers and grown-up readers at work. Just make sure the book being discussed is suitable for your age group. Also ask the librarian if any authors are in town. You might get to go to a book signing! You might meet someone famous...

10 Creative Writing Exercises

Here are ten creative writing exercises for you to try. I've started a story for you. All you have to do is develop the idea into a finished story. Or you could practise writing a beginning, a middle or end. You can use these ideas to practise everything I've told you, for example, pick an exercise and develop a character for it.

Only practise one tip at a time e.g. just focus on setting, then start a new story and just focus on writing the beginning, etc. If you focus on too much at once, you'll feel overwhelmed.

Here are summaries of the exercises. It doesn't matter which order you go in:

Exercise 1: A desert island and a pirate ship...

Exercise 2: School's out! It's snowing! A week off! Woohoo!

Exercise 3: Locked in a theme park. At night. Alone...

Exercise 4: Help! A witch turned me into an animal!

Exercise 5: There's an alien in the basement!

Exercise 6: A television sucked in your family! Off to the rescue!

Exercise 7: Stuck in a haunted house on Halloween...

Exercise 8: Two kids lost in the jungle. How will they get home?

Exercise 9: A boy wakes up with magical powers!

Exercise 10: A girl swaps bodies with someone famous. How can she switch back?

You can start writing using those summaries or continue reading for detailed versions. Feel free to change any details you like. It's your story and your rules.

Exercise 1: A desert island and a pirate ship...

A boy was on a cruise ship with his family. When they stopped by a desert island, the boy jumped off for a swim. He didn't tell anyone he'd left. Unfortunately, the ship left him behind. Stuck on a desert island, he's got to find a way back to the ship. Then a pirate ship shows up...

Exercise 2: School's out! It's snowing! A week off! Woohoo!

Oh no! School is flooded. Classes are cancelled. Now hundreds of kids have no homework and nothing else to do. Then it snows...

Exercise 3: Locked in a theme park. At night. Alone...

A group of school kids got lost in a theme park. The park attendant didn't notice, so he's locked up for the night. Now they're stuck in a theme park! Luckily the attendant left all the rides running...

Exercise 4: Help! A witch turned me into an animal!

A little girl was rude to an old woman in the street. Oops! The woman turns out to be a witch. The witch casts a spell that turns the girl into an animal and leaves the poor girl in her garden. Then her parents come home...

Exercise 5: There's an alien in the basement. What should he say to it?

A little boy hears a bump in the night. He goes to his parents' room but they don't want to get out of bed. His older brother and sister kicked him out their rooms. He's got no choice but to check out downstairs himself. He goes down and finds an alien in the basement. And it can talk! What should he say to it? What will it say to him?

Exercise 6: The television sucked in her family. What should she do?

A little girl was spending Saturday afternoon in front of the TV with her parents. When she went to get another drink, she heard a loud bang. She ran back to the living room. Her family had vanished! Then she turns and sees them stuck in the TV...

Exercise 7: Stuck in a haunted house on Halloween. Help!

Twin boys ignored their mum. They went in a haunted house when they were supposed to have gone back to the car. Now they're locked in the biggest haunted house in the world, at night, on Halloween. Will they survive the night? If the ghosts and monsters let them...

Exercise 8: Two kids lost in the jungle. How will they get home?

Twin girls went out camping with their older brother. After an argument, they ran off. Now they're lost in the jungle and it's getting dark. If they don't find their brother soon, they'll have to spend a night in the deadliest jungle in the world...

Exercise 9: A boy wakes up with magical powers!

A boy wakes up for school. The day starts like any other: eat breakfast, brush teeth, shower, get dressed, and make the cat disappear? Huh? Yep. He's got magical powers. It must be the flu he had last week. Armed with magical powers, today will be the best school day ever!

Exercise 10: A girl swaps bodies with someone famous. How can she switch back?

A girl swaps places with someone really famous. Now she's got lots of money and lots of power. No wonder she doesn't want her old life back! But then she sees the darker side of fame. She doesn't like it! Is it too late to go back home?

Keep practising those exercises and then think of your own. You don't even have to start with a paragraph like I did. Try writing a story from one word. It's fun to see what you come up with. Here are words to experiment with:

Vampire
Apple
Sunrise
Mars
Ice
Computer
Angels
TV
Rats
Fire
Oceans
Love
Best friends
Wool
Aliens
Ninja
Family
Author
Puppy
Kitten
Rabbit

Cheese
Moon
Sun
Forest
Cupcakes
Winter
Summer
Rain
Boy
Girl
Rainbow
Dreams
Monster
Homework
Classroom
Ice cream
Sugar
Banana
Orange
Grapes
Book
Pen
Paint
Holiday/Vacation
Train
Bus
Race car
Butter
Dance
Drums

See? Just pick a word and see what you come up with. It might be a novel, a short story, or even a poem. It doesn't matter. Just write and see what happens. If you don't like any of these words, write down your own and start from there.

Well, I've told you everything I know. Now it's time to say goodbye...

The End

The writers who last a lifetime have lots of books. Readers will want more from you because you'll get better and better. Because writing is so fun, you'll love writing lots of stories.

For the next couple of years, you're going to focus just on writing. Keep trying different genres - adventure, fantasy, mystery, horror and much more. You can always do more than one. I do. Then you'll have fun choosing different pen names. Mine are Zada Green, Zia Black, and Zhané White. They're for adults, so read them when you're older.

See how fun being a writer is? Different stories, different names, different readers.

And it all starts with lots of practise.

So get going!

Dear Reader

Hello, I hope you enjoyed my work. Now the book is over, here are three things to consider. It'll only take around five minutes, and I'd really appreciate you taking a look.

1. An honest review.

Could you do me a favour? I'd really appreciate a review. Whether you loved it, hated it, or thought my book was just okay, it doesn't matter. Just be honest. It doesn't have to be a long review, just a brief summary of what you thought. Thank you very much!

2. Exclusive subscriber goodies.

I have a mailing list on my website: www.zuniblue.com. All subscribers will be the first to know when I publish a new book. Also, you'll know whenever my books are sold as a box set, discounted, or available for free. If you want to send me a message back, email me at contact@zuniblue.com. I respond to everyone.

3. Keep reading!

If you enjoyed this book, why not try another? Here's what I recommend:

The Mean Girl Who Never Speaks
The Mya Dove Case Files start with The Mean Girl Who Never Speaks, a crime short story. There's a new girl at school. Rumour has it she doesn't speak, doesn't smile much, and doesn't play with others. That means she's mean, right? Maybe. Maybe not...

About the Author

Zuni Blue's been telling tales since she was a kid. Now she gets to mix fun stories with a few lessons learnt on the way to adulthood. Whether it's solving cases at school or fighting monsters, Zuni promises a great read you'll never forget!

Pen Names:
Zia Black www.ziablack.com (crime and thrillers)
Zhané White www.zhanewhite.com (fantasy and science fiction)
Zada Green www.zadagreen.com (sarcastic self-help and general fiction)
Zuni Blue www.zuniblue.com (children's books)

Dedications

To my younger self, who used to write short stories in a notebook. All that practise paid off! Thank you to my family. I appreciate all the love and support you have given over the years and in the future. Also, thanks to great readers like you. Enjoy all my stories!

Made in the USA
Monee, IL
02 August 2023

40338122R00025